Praise for
THE BLUEFISH COOKBOOK

"Excellent recipes. Splendid instructions."   **—The New York Times**

"Charming . . . obviously a labor of love."   **—Bon Appetit**

"The most complete collection of bluefish recipes around, ranging from simple to elaborate to the somewhat wacky."
—The Boston Globe

"A truly superior little cookbook."   **—The Martha's Vineyard Times**

"Each year bluefish explode along the eastern seaboard . . . soon everyone is up to his boots in bluefish. The first few taste wonderful. The second taste almost as good . . . but pretty soon the bluefish blahs begin to set in. To the rescue come the authors of *The Bluefish Cook-book* with recipes ranging from Bluefish Hash, Bluefish with Gin, to salads, cakes and chowders. . . . This is a book with salt breezes blowing through the pages—a fine cookbook done by two who know their blues."   **—Seafood Leader**

THE BLUEFISH COOKBOOK

Greta Jacobs & Jane Alexander

Third Edition, Revised and Expanded

Illustrated by Wezi Swift

The Globe Pequot Press

138 West Main Street
Chester, Connecticut 06412

Manufactured in the United States of America

ISBN: 0-87106-804-4
Library of Congress Catalogue Number: 79-51760

Third Edition/Second Printing, 1987

" WE CONTEMPLATED CALLING THIS BOOK "WHAT TO DO WHEN YOU'VE GOT THE BLUES," BECAUSE WHEN THE BLUEFISH ARE RUNNING OFF THE ATLANTIC COAST AND THERE ARE FISHERPERSONS AMONG YOUR FAMILY OR FRIENDS, BLUEFISH CAN BECOME A STAPLE OF YOUR DAILY DIET. THE FILLETS ARE DELICIOUS SIMPLY BAKED WITH SALT AND PEPPER AND DOTTED WITH BUTTER. KNOWING HOW WONDERFULLY SPECIAL THIS FINE FISH TASTES, AFTER YEARS OF PREPARING THEM A VARIETY OF WAYS, WE THOUGHT WE'D SHARE SOME OF OUR EXPERIENCE. WE ARE GRATEFUL TO OUR FRIENDS FOR INCLUDING SOME OF THEIR FAVORITE RECIPES TOO.

MOST OF THE RECIPES CALL FOR THE FILLETS OF THE FISH, WHICH WE FEEL ARE SUPERIOR TO THE WHOLE FISH IN COOKING. IF YOU DO NOT KNOW HOW TO FILLET WE SUGGEST YOU ASK SOMEONE WHO DOES.

DO NOT WASH THE FILLETS BEFORE COOKING; TO PRESERVE FLAVOR PAT THEM DRY WITH PAPER TOWELS.

BECAUSE BLUEFISH USUALLY WEIGH BETWEEN TWO AND FIFTEEN POUNDS, THE NUMBER OF PORTIONS YOU CAN SERVE WILL DEPEND ON THE SIZE OF YOUR FISH. THE FILLETS FROM

A SIX-POUND FISH WILL SERVE FOUR GENEROUSLY.

IN POACHING THE FISH A GOOD RULE OF THUMB FOR COOKING TIME IS TEN MINUTES PER INCH THICKNESS OF FISH AT ITS THICKEST PART. WHEN BAKING IT IS WISEST TO INCREASE THE TIME TO FIFTEEN TO TWENTY MINUTES PER INCH AT 375° OR UNTIL THE FISH IS JUST COOKED THROUGH, AND NO MORE.

AND, LASTLY, TO AID IN YOUR CLEAN-UP, BAKE THE FISH ON A SHEET OF FOIL IF YOU ARE USING A METAL PAN.

BON APPÉTIT.

GRETA JACOBS
JANE ALEXANDER

NANTUCKET

SWEET AND SOUR BLUES

2 FILLETS - CUT INTO 3x3" PIECES

~ SAUCE

1/2 CUP SUGAR	4 TBS SOY SAUCE
1/3 CUP VINEGAR	2 CUPS WATER
3 TBS SHERRY	4 TBS CORNSTARCH
	1 YSP SALT

4 TBS GINGER - MINCED
3 SCALLIONS - CHOPPED

MIX ALL INGREDIENTS FOR SAUCE, EXCEPT GINGER & SCALLIONS. DREDGE FISH IN FLOUR. FRY IN VERY HOT OIL, 1/2" DEEP, IN A LARGE SKILLET - FOR 2 MIN. EACH SIDE. LOWER HEAT AND COOK 2 MIN. MORE EACH SIDE. RAISE HEAT AND COOK 1 MIN. MORE EACH SIDE. THE FISH SHOULD BE QUITE CRISP NOW. KEEP WARM IN 150° OVEN, BUT NO LONGER THAN 10 MIN. OR FISH WILL LOSE IT'S CRISPNESS. POUR OFF ALL BUT 1 TBS OIL. SAUTÉ GINGER & SCALLIONS. ADD SAUCE & COOK UNTIL TRANSLUCENT, 3-5 MIN. POUR OVER FISH & SERVE.

BLUEFISH BAKED IN CREAM

2 FILLETS
3/4 CUP HEAVY CREAM
   BUTTER
   CHOPPED PARSLEY
  SALT AND PEPPER

PREHEAT OVEN TO 375.°

Place bluefish skin side down, on a greased baking dish. DOT WITH BUTTER AND BAKE ABOUT 15 MINUTES. Add CREAM AND BAKE 10 MINUTES MORE - BASTING WITH PAN JUICES. SEASON WITH SALT and PEPPER. SERVE WITH Chopped parsley AND PAN JUICES.

BRIAN'S BLUES

2 FILLETS
1/3 CUP BUTTER
1 tsp Fresh garlic - DICED
1 CUP imPORTED BEER
   CORNSTARCH

3 TBS HEAVY CREAM
2 tsp BASIL
1 tsp PAPRIKA
   SALT & PEPPER
BROWN RICE - COOKED

RUB FILLETS WITH SALT & PEPPER, LET STAND A
FEW MINUTES. HEAT BUTTER IN A LARGE SKILLET.
ADD GARLIC and HEAT UNTIL garlic SIZZLES.
ADD BEER and bring TO a SIMMER. ADD FISH,
SKIN SIDE DOWN. COVER. BASTE FREQUENTLY.
WHEN FISH is DONE PLACE ON A BED OF BROWN
RICE. ADD CREAM and SEASONINGS to JUICES IN
PAN. THICKEN WITH A FEW SPRINKLES OF CORN-
STARCH. POUR OVER FILLETS and SPRINKLE WITH
PAPRIKA.

HONEY - DIPPED BLUEFISH CHEEKS

½ CUP BUTTER

1-2 Lbs. Fresh BLUEFISH CHEEKS

¾ CUP White Flour

¼ CUP CORN MEAL

½ Fresh LEMON

3 TBS HONEY

2 EGGS

1 TBS WATER

2 TBS Fresh MINT

HEAT butter over low FLAME IN HEAVY Frying Pan. Do not allow to burn. Place Cheeks in Colander and SQUEEZE the lemon over them - Drain - (Do not rinse with water. It will destroy the Flavor). Lightly BEAT EGGS & water & HONEY in A Flat bowl. Fill a brown Paper bag with flour and corn meal. COAT CHEEKS with Honey mixture and shake in bag of flour and cornmeal. Fry in the butter (Just below the burning point) until golden brown - turning only once. Drain on paper towel. Serve Hot, sprinkled with mint and lemon juice.

NOTES:

Some people like a heavy batter, therefore double dipping is suggested. Bluefish cheeks are the most DELECTABLE part of the fish and usually sell for much less than the fillets. You may also use this RECIPE on fillets cut into finger-size pieces for fish sticks or into bite-size pieces for Hors d'oeuvres.

Jean's Bluefish with Sour Cream

2 FILLETS	1/2 CUP MAYONNAISE
SALT and PEPPER	3 TBS CHOPPED CHIVES
1 1/2 CUPS SOUR CREAM	3 TBS LEMON JUICE

PREHEAT OVEN TO 375°.

Dry FILLETS AND RUB with SALT and PEPPER. Arrange in buttered casserole (preferably an earthenware baking dish). mix cream, mayonnaise chives and lemon juice. Season with salt and pepper. spread over fillets. Bake 20 minutes. Place under broiler to brown.

Liz's Bluefish Pudding - Nordic Style

2 Fillets
1 Cup Rice - Converted
2 Cups milk
3 Eggs

3 Cups Half & Half
  Bay Leaf
1 TBS Worcestershire
1/2 tsp Grated Nutmeg

PREHEAT OVEN TO 350°

Heat the Half & Half with 1 tsp salt, bay Leaf and the Worcestershire sauce. Add the Fillets, cover and simmer slowly for 20 minutes or until Fish is Flaky and tender. Allow Fish to cool in the sauce.

    Meanwhile bring the milk to almost a boil in the top of a Double Boiler. Add the rice, reduce the heat and cook for 25 min. or until most of the milk is absorbed. Blend the eggs with the rice, adding the nutmeg and 1 cup of the liquid in which the Fish was cooked. Bone and Flake the fish Finely and

add to the Rice mixture. Place in a well-greased baking dish. Bake for 50-60 minutes.
Serve with Lignon berries or whole cranberry sauce.

MOUSSE DE BLUEFISH

1 1/2 lbs. BLUEFISH – COOKED
2 CUPS LIGHT CREAM
5 EGGS
4 EGG WHITES

2 TBS BUTTER – MELTED
SALT & WHITE PEPPER
3 CUPS HOLLANDAISE
(SEE SAUCES)

PREHEAT OVEN TO 350°.

In a blender combine fillets, eggs, egg whites, butter and half the cream. Blend until smooth. Combine with rest of cream. Add salt and pepper and transfer to a 2qt. casserole place in a pan of water and bake uncovered for 45 minutes or until a knife inserted in center comes out clean. Serve with Hollandaise sauce.

FRENCH BLUE SANDWICH

BLUEFISH SALAD (SEE PAGE 22 - OMIT ALFALFA SPROUTS)
8 SLICES OF BREAD - 4 SANDWICHES
2 EGGS
1/4 CUP CREAM
PINCH OF NUTMEG
SALT & PEPPER
BUTTER

Make four sandwiches from the BLUEFISH SALAD. BEAT the EGGS slightly with the CREAM, and add the seasonings. Dip sandwiches in the EGG mixture. FRY IN BUTTER UNTIL golden on BOTH sides.

SERVES 4

BLUEFISH FLORENTINE

1 1/2 cups puréed spinach or 2 boxes frozen
chopped spinach
2 fillets
flour 2 TBS olive oil
salt & pepper mornay sauce
parmesan cheese

HEAT OIL IN FRYING PAN. DIP FILLETS IN SEASONED
FLOUR AND BROWN IN OIL ON BOTH SIDES. Place
SPINACH IN A GREASED shallow baking dish. Place
FILLETS ON TOP OF SPINACH. COVER WITH MORNAY sauce
and SPRINKLE with PARMESAN CHEESE. BROIL UNTIL
CHEESE is bubbly.

~ MORNAY SAUCE

2 TBS BUTTER 3/4 cup CREAM
1 1/2 TBS FLOUR 1 EGG YOLK - beaten
PINCH OF NUTMEG, SALT & PEPPER

OVER MEDIUM HEAT MELT BUTTER and add FLOUR. STIR A
FEW MINUTES, THEN gradually Add CREAM. STIR UNTIL thick-
ENED. Add SEASONINGS. Add a SMALL AMOUNT OF SAUCE to
THE EGG YOLK, THEN RETURN mixture to THE SAUCE, UNTIL HEATED.

SMOKED BLUEFISH

2 FILLETS
SALT and PEPPER
Woodchips (Preferably Hickory)

Soak the woodchips overnight in water. Place a double layer of charcoal in the fire pit of your smoker and burn until gray. Put a single layer of chips on the coals and wait until they are smoking well. Place a pan of water over the coals and smoking chips. And place the seasoned fillets, skin side down, on the grill in the smoker. Cover and smoke at least 8 hours. Approximately every two hours stir coals and place another layer of chips on.

If you have no commercially made smoker, take a metal garbage can and fill the bottom with 1-inch layer of sand. At the

TOP LEVEL OF SAND - PUNCH FOUR HOLES, THE SIZE OF DIMES, IN THE CAN. PLACE THE COALS ON THE SAND. PIERCE SIDES OF THE CAN ABOUT A FOOT ABOVE THE bed of COALS AND PUT 2 METAL RODS through the CAN, to PROVIDE SUPPORT FOR the METAL BASIN OF WATER. REPEAT SAME, FOR SUPPORT FOR YOUR GRILL - 8-10 INCHES ABOVE WATER BASIN. USE THE CAN COVER AS A TOP. THE WATER KEEPS the FISH COOL and moist WHILE the SMOKE HAS ITS EFFECT ON THE MEAT.

** FOR A SUPERB, DRYER SMOKED FISH SOAK the FILLETS OVER NIGHT, IN A glass or CERAMIC DISH, IN JOHN'S BRINE.

BRINE

2 QUARTS WATER	½ CUP LEMON JUICE
1 CUP NON- IODIZED SALT	¼ TBS GARLIC POWDER
½ CUP BROWN SUGAR	1 tsp ONION POWDER

AFTER SOAKING IN THE BRINE WASH the FILLETS Thoroughly IN WATER and PAT DRY BEFORE SMOKING.

COLD BLUEFISH POACHED WITH SORREL SAUCE

2 FILLETS
SORREL SAUCE
(SEE SAUCES)

Wrap each fillet in Reynolds wrap and place in a large skillet over medium HEAT. Add enough water to the pan to barely cover fillets. Cover skillet and bring water to A boil. Reduce HEAT and simmer for About 20-25 minutes. Serve cold with sorrel sauce.

Great for a luncheon or summer supper.

BLUEFISH WITH GIN

2 FILLETS
½ CUP GIN

PREHEAT OVEN TO 375°.

Place Fillets in buttered casserole. Cover with gin.
Bake For 20 minutes.

BLUEFISH FRITTERS

2 CUPS COOKED FISH- CHOPPED FINE
1 ONION - MINCED
1 TBS MELTED BUTTER
1 EGG - BEATEN SLIGHTLY
1/2 tsp baking powder
  FLOUR (ABOUT 1/2 CUP)
  OIL FOR FRYING
  CLAM BROTH - optional

MIX ALL INGREDIENTS, USING ENOUGH FLOUR TO HOLD TOGETHER (IF NECESSARY TO THIN, USE CLAM BROTH OR FISH STOCK). REFRIGERATE FOR AN HOUR. DROP TABLESPOONS OF BATTER INTO 1/2" OF HOT OIL, IN A HEAVY FRYING PAN (OR DEEP FRY). FRY SLOWLY, TURNING ONCE. DRAIN ON A PAPER TOWEL AND KEEP WARM.

SERVE WITH CATSUP.

BLUEFISH Andros Island STYLE

2 FILLETS

24 ozs Clam BROth or
      Fish STOCK

1 CARROT

1 BAY LEAF

½ cup White WINE

½ cup White UINEGAR

3 LEMONS

3 EGG YOLKS

In a fish poacher or kettle bring the broth, carrot, bay leaf, wine and vinegar to a boil. Add the fillets (no need for a rack) and enough water to barely cover the fish. Cover and poach for 10-15 minutes (10 minutes per inch thickness of fillet at the thickest part). Beat the egg yolks in a bowl until frothy. Add the juice of the 3 lemons. Remove the fish from the broth, cut into about six pieces and place in a soup tureen. Add a few tablespoons of the broth to the egg mixture- to be sure the egg won't cook in the Hot liquid. Then stir all the broth and Egg mixture together and pour over the fish. Serve immediately in large soup bowls and accompany with french bread. Do not reheat as Egg will become cooked.

BLUEFISH WITH MUSTARD

2 FILLETS
DIJON MUSTARD

PREHEAT OVEN TO 375°.

Place fish in greased baking dish. Spread a generous (do not skimp) coat of mustard over top of fillets. Bake for 20 minutes or until fish flakes easily with a fork.

LEMON and GARLIC BLUES

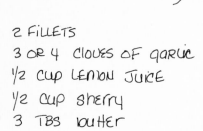

2 FILLETS
3 OR 4 CLOVES OF garlic
1/2 CUP LEMON JUICE
1/2 CUP sherry
3 TBS butter

PREHEAT OVEN TO 375°.

PRESS the garlic cloves and add the fine pressings to the lemon juice and sherry. marinate the fillets in this mixture for 15 minutes. Then bake the fillets for 20-25 minutes. simmer the marinade in a saucepan for several minutes to cook the garlic. Add the butter and pour the sauce over fillets just before serving.

COLD POACHED WHOLE BLUEFISH

1 WHOLE BLUEFISH, 4-5 lbs.	2 RIBS CELERY
2 CUPS WHITE VINEGAR	1 tsp DILL
2 CUPS DRY WHITE WINE	2 tsp MIXED HERBS
2 CARROTS	CLOVES

IN Fish Poacher (or Kettle with a rack on the bottom, large enough for length of fish). Wrap fish in cheesecloth and put aside. Boil other ingredients with about 3 quarts of water covered for 20 minutes. Add fish, in cheesecloth, for easy removal. Cover and simmer until done, about 20 minutes. Remove fish and carefully peel away skin. Cover with plastic wrap and refrigerate several hours. Serve surrounded by cold cooked vegetables and a choice of sauce.

ED'S BLUEFISH SALAD

1 FILLET, COOKED & FLAKED
2 RIBS CELERY
3 SCALLIONS

1 CUP ALFALFA SPROUTS
SALT & PEPPER
TOMATO YOGURT SAUCE
(SEE SAUCES)

Dice the scallions and celery and mix with other ingredients. Season to taste. Serve in scooped-out tomatoes on a bed of lettuce or as a sandwich on dark bread. May also be used as canapés on small toasted rounds or crackers.

BLUE ON BLUE

2 FILLETS
1/4 Lb BLUE CHEESE - CRUMBLED
1/2 cup fine Bread crumbs

PREHEAT OVEN TO 375°.

Place fillets in a greased shallow baking pan.
BAKE FOR 10 MINUTES. REMOVE FROM OVEN.
COVER FILLETS with the CHEESE and TOP WITH the
BREAD CRUMBS. BAKE ANOTHER 10-15 MINUTES OR
UNTIL fillets are TENDER and CHEESE is MELTED.

WENDY'S BLUEFISH WITH SOY SAUCE

2 FILLETS
1 MEDIUM ONION - SLICED
1/8 CUP SOY SAUCE
1 CAN WHOLE TOMATOES

JUICE OF 1/2 A LEMON
2 tsp MIXED HERBS
1/2 GREEN PEPPER- SLICED
1/3 CUP PITTED BLACK OLIVES

PREHEAT OVEN TO 375°

Line a shallow baking dish with sliced onions.
Place fillets, skin side down, on onions. Rub soy
sauce into fillets. Arrange tomatoes, cut in half,
green peppers and olives on top of fillets. Pour
1/2 of the tomato juice over fish. Squeeze the
lemon over all and season to taste. Bake
15 - 20 minutes.

PLANKED BLUEFISH - CONNECTICUT RIVER STYLE

FISH FILLETS
BACON
PAPRIKA

SAUCE

2 PARTS OLIVE OIL   GARLIC (OPTIONAL)
1 PART LEMON JUICE   SALT + PEPPER
      OR ANY BOTTLED OIL & VINEGAR DRESSING

THESE BLUEFISH ARE BAKED IN FRONT OF AN OPEN
FIRE, GREAT FOR A COOKOUT. LAY FILLETS ON AN
OAK BOARD, OR ANY OTHER HARDWOOD (DO NOT USE
PINE OR ANY SOFTWOODS). TOP EACH FILLET WITH A
SLICE OF BACON. USING LARGE HEAD NAILS ABOUT
1½" IN LENGTH (ROOFING NAILS WORK WELL) NAIL THE
FILLETS TO THE BOARD, SECURING THE BACON. NAIL
TWO NAILS IN THE TOP AND TWO IN THE BOTTOM.

leave enough of the nail Heads out that they can be easily removed. Brush each fillet generously with the sauce and sprinkle each with paprika. When the fire is roaring place the boards about 18" away and at a 60° angle away from the fire. Cook for 40 minutes, turning board upside-down after 20 minutes. Denail fillets with the claw of A Hammer, being careful not to burn fingers on the hot boards. Wear heavy mits.

BLUEFISH STEAKS

1½" THICK STEAKS - CUT ACROSS THE SPINE OF A FRESH BLUEFISH - LIKE SALMON STEAKS
SALT & freshly ground Pepper

Place steaks in a 2-sided Hamburger grill and cook over charcoal until golden brown. Cook about 15 minutes each side, turning constantly to prevent burning.

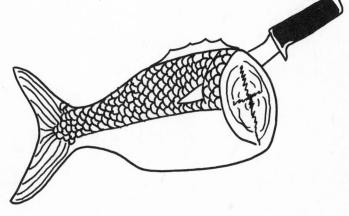

BLUEFISH WITH SHALLOT BUTTER AND PINE NUTS

2 FILLETS
1/8 LB BUTTER (1/2 A STICK) - SOFTENED
3 TBS SHALLOTS - FINELY CHOPPED
2 TBS PINE NUTS
1/2 CUP FINE BREAD CRUMBS
   SALT & PEPPER

PREHEAT OVEN TO 375.°

MIX SOFTENED BUTTER WITH THE SHALLOTS, PARSLEY,
PINE NUTS, BREAD CRUMBS, SALT AND PEPPER.
COVER FILLETS WITH THIS MIXTURE AND BAKE
20 - 25 MINUTES.

   SERVE WITH LEMON WEDGES.

                              SERVES 5-6

Ruth's Rice stuffed whole Bluefish

1 whole Bluefish 4-5 lbs
2 cups rice
4 cups clam broth
2 TBS Butter
1 cup seedless currants - soaked in 1/2 cup white
1/2 cup pinenuts or sunflower seeds.   wine.

3 TBS Parsley - chopped
3 TBS Dill - chopped
1 cup onion - chopped
1 cup celery - chopped fine

Basting Liquid

Juice of 1 Lemon
1 cup white wine
1/2 cup olive oil

2 TBS Parsley
2 TBS Dill

PREHEAT OVEN TO 375°

Cook rice in clam broth. Sauté onions, celery,
dill, and parsley in butter until tender. mix
in rice, currants and nuts. Stuff fish. Place any
leftover stuffing in a separate casserole dish.
Skewer fish and lace closed. Place in pan and pour

basting liquid over fish. Bake for an hour. Place the extra stuffing in the oven at the same time and serve with the fish.

BLUEFISH DIFFERENT

2 FILLETS

Wrap bluefish fillets separately and tightly in foil. Place wrapped fish in upper rack of dishwasher. Use no soap but run washer through its complete cycle.
Serve with tartar sauce and lemon wedges.

FISHERMAN BILL'S FAVORITE

2 FILLETS - WITH DARK MEAT REMOVED
3 ONIONS - SLICED
1 CAN CREAM OF CELERY SOUP - UNDILUTED

PREHEAT OVEN TO 375°

PLACE SLICED ONIONS ON THE BOTTOM OF A
BUTTERED CASSEROLE OR BAKING DISH. LAY
FILLETS ON TOP OF ONIONS AND COVER WITH
THE CELERY SOUP. BAKE FOR 20 MINUTES OR
UNTIL FISH FLAKES EASILY WITH A FORK.

BLUEFISH CAKES

1 FILLET - COOKED & FLAKED
4 MEDIUM POTATOES
2 ONIONS
2 EGGS   SALT + PEPPER
2/3 CUP MAYONNAISE   BUTTER OR VEG. OIL

PEEL, COOK, AND MASH POTATOES. CHOP ONIONS AND
SAUTÉ THEM IN BUTTER OR OIL UNTIL GOLDEN. MIX
FISH, POTATOES, ONIONS, EGGS, MAYONNAISE AND
SPICES TOGETHER. FORM INTO PATTIES. COOK IN
FRYING PAN IN BUTTER OR OIL UNTIL BROWN, TURNING
ONCE. SERVE WITH TOMATO-YOGURT SAUCE OR
KETCHUP.

WHEN FORMED INTO BITE-SIZE BALLS MAY BE
SERVED AS CANAPÉS WITH CHOICE OF SAUCE.

BLUEFISH WITH TOPPING

2 FILLETS
½ LEMON

SHREDDED WHEAT
BUTTER

PREHEAT OVEN TO 375°.

SQUEEZE LEMON OVER FILLETS. PLACE IN GREASED
BAKING DISH. GRIND SHREDDED WHEAT IN A
BLENDER (OR PULVERIZE WITH A ROLLING PIN). MAKE
ENOUGH CRUMBS TO MAKE A GENEROUS TOPPING.
PLACE OVER FILLETS. DOT WITH BUTTER. BAKE 20
MINUTES OR UNTIL FISH FLAKES EASILY WITH A
FORK. SERVE WITH LEMON WEDGES AND PARSLEY.

COLD CURED BLUEFISH OR BLOX

2 FRESH FILLETS	2 TBS GROUND PEPPER
4 BUNCHES OF DILL	2/3 CUP SALT
2 TBS GROUND ALLSPICE	2/3 CUP SUGAR

Rub the flesh of the fillets thoroughly with salt, sugar and allspice. Place one FILLET, SKIN side down, on a bed of DILL in a glass or ceramic dish or platter which has sides at least 1/2 inch high. Cover with DILL and place the SECOND FILLET FLESH side down on top to make a sandwich. SPRINKLE with remaining salt mixture and cover with the rest of the DILL. Cover platter with plastic wrap. Place a board on top and additional weights as well (such as stones) and refrigerate for at least 48 hours but preferably 3-4 days.

TURN THE SANDWICH ONCE EVERY 12 HOURS. DO
NOT DISCARD THE JUICE AS IT AIDS IN THE
CURING. WHEN READY TO SERVE, DISCARD THE
JUICE AND DILL AND SCRAPE THE SPICES OFF THE
FLESH. SLICE THINLY AND HORIZONTALLY TO THE
SKIN. SERVE AS YOU WOULD LOX, WITH CREAM
CHEESE, BAGELS OR DARK BREAD, LEMON WEDGES
AND/OR MUSTARD DILL SAUCE (SEE SAUCES) OR
AS CANAPÉS ON SMALL TOASTED ROUNDS.

EASY BLUEFISH Custard PIE

makes its own crust. Is lighter and more tender than a quiche. DELICIOUS FOR A quickie lunch or supper.

½ cup COOKED BLUEFISH - Cut in small pieces.
1 small green pepper - SEEDED & chopped
1 small ONION - chopped
1 CLOVE garlic - minced
8-10 mushrooms - SLICED
1 TBS Butter
½ cup Bisquick
1½ cups milk

3 EGGS
2 TBS SOFT Butter

PREHEAT OVEN TO 375°.

Sauté green peppers & onions in 1 TBS Butter until limp. Add garlic & mushrooms and sauté a few minutes longer. Add fish.

Put Bisquick, milk, eggs and SOFT BUTTER in the blender. mix by pushing the First button ON - THEN OFF. DO NOT OVER-mix. Add Fish & VEGETABLES to blender mixture AND pour into A GREASED 10" PIE PLATE. BAKE For 30 minutes or UNTIL custard is SET. LET STAND 5 minutes before serving.

BLUEFISH STEW

1 MEDIUM BLUEFISH OR 2 FILLETS	1 CUP COOKED CORN NIBLETS
2 SMALL ONIONS - chopped	1 CUP COOKED lima BEANS
2 TBS FLOUR	SALT & PEPPER
2 TBS BUTTER	WORCESTERSHIRE SAUCE
2 CANS EVAPORATED MILK	1 TBS LEMON JUICE
2 CUPS MILK	

Simmer fish in the 2 cups of milk until white and flaky. Remove from pan, reserving liquid, and cut into bite-size pieces. Discard skin and black meat. In a stew pot sauté onions in the butter until golden. Add flour, stir, then gradually add liquid from the cooked fish; the evaporated milk and the fish pieces. Simmer ten minutes. Add corn, lima beans and seasonings. Simmer 10 minutes more.

Serve in bowls with oyster crackers.

Honey Blues

2 Fillets
½ cup lemon juice
½ cup honey
1½ oz. sliced Almonds

Preheat oven to 375.°

Marinate the fillets in the mixed honey, lemon juice and almonds for 15 minutes. Bake the fillets for 20-25 minutes, then place under the broiler for a minute to brown the almonds. Just before serving, heat the reserved marinade and pour over the fillets.

ITALIAN STYLE BAKED BLUEFISH

2 FILLETS
1 1/2 lbs POTATOES
2/3 CUP OLIVE OIL

1 TBS garlic- CHOPPED
1/4 CUP PARSLEY- CHOPPED
SALT & PEPPER

PREHEAT OVEN TO 450°

Peel and slice potatoes. Use a shallow casserole, but large enough to accommodate fish without over lapping. Put in potatoes and half the olive oil, half the garlic, half the parsley and salt and pepper to taste. Mix well. Spread potatoes evenly to cover dish. Place on the upper rack and bake until potatoes are half done- about 15 minutes. Remove from oven and place fish, skin side down, over potatoes. Baste fish with remaining oil, garlic, parsley and salt and pepper. Return to oven and bake for ten minutes more.

Remove from oven and baste with pan juices.
Return again to oven for another Ten minutes
or until fish is flaky and Potatoes are
browned.

Blinns & Blues

2 smoked fillets
  milk
  Lemon Juice
  Parsley - Chopped

CREAM sauce
  3 TBS Butter
  3 TBS Flour
  1 cup milk or cream

In a sauce pan barely cover fillets with milk. Bring milk to almost a boil. Reduce Heat and simmer until tender. Make the cream sauce in the top of a double Boiler. Flake the fillets with a fork and remove any bones. Add to the cream sauce. Heat, sprinkle with lemon Juice and parsley to taste.

Serve on Toast points or Rice.

Small Blues Sautéed with Bacon and Onions

2 small Fillets - 3 lbs or more
4 strips of Bacon
4 scallions - chopped
   milk
   Flour (CORN MEAL)
   Salt & Pepper

In a large frying pan cook bacon until crisp.
Remove, crumble and keep warm. Cook scallions
in bacon grease until limp. Remove and keep
warm. Dip fillets first in the milk then in
the seasoned flour (or ½ flour, ½ corn meal).
Fry in the bacon grease about 3 minutes on
one side, turn and cook 3 minutes on the
other side, or until nicely browned. Top with
bacon and onions, serve.

DEVILISH BLUES

2 FILLETS
 MELTED BUTTER
1 CUP GRATED CHEDDAR CHEESE
⅛ tsp tabasco
1 TBS PREPARED MUSTARD
1 TBS HORSERADISH

BRUSH FILLETS WITH MELTED BUTTER. BROIL 10
MINUTES. MIX ALL OTHER INGREDIENTS. COAT
FILLETS WITH MIXTURE AND RETURN TO BROILER
UNTIL CHEESE IS MELTED AND BROWNED.

SMOKED BLUEFISH PÂTÉ

4 OZ. SMOKED FISH
4 OZ. CREAM CHEESE
1 SMALL ONION - CHOPPED FINE
1 1/2 TBS LEMON JUICE

Combine all the ingredients in a blender and blend until smooth. Garnish with a few sprigs of parsley and serve on crackers or melba toast.

BLUEFISH CHOWDER

1 LARGE BLUEFISH OR 2 FILLETS
1 CARROT   2 CELERY STALKS
1 ONION - QUARTERED   3 ONIONS CHOPPED
1/2 lb. BACON OR 1/4 lb. SALT PORK
5 MEDIUM POTATOES PEELED & QUARTERED
1 CUP CREAM
  PAPRIKA

Poach fish in water to barely cover fillets.
Add the carrot, cut up, the onion, quartered and
the celery stalks. Cook for 25-30 minutes or
till fish is flaky. Strain, reserve stock
(About 4 cups). Remove fish from bones,
discarding bones and skin. Sauté chopped bacon
or pork in frying pan till golden. Add chopped
onions and sauté till golden. Remove from heat.
Cook potatoes in stock until just tender. Cut

Potatoes into serving size pieces. Add fish, onions and bacon. Cook over low heat. Add cream and salt and pepper to taste. Do Not allow to boil. Serve in a bowl with a pat of butter and a dash of Paprika. For a richer chowder use evaporated milk.

Fish Stock

1 Bluefish carcass - with head and tail after
1/2 cup white vinegar   filleting.
1/2 cup white wine
2 carrots
2 ribs celery
1 TBS dill - chopped or seeds
2 QTS water

Simmer carcass in water with other ingredients
for 30-40 minutes. Uncover and strain, discarding
bones. Boil down stock, uncovered, for another
1/2 hour or until 2/3 of the amount is left.
This stock will keep in the refrigerator for 2
weeks if boiled every few days and is a good
base for sauces, soups and Bouillabaisse. The
gel from the stock is good by itself eaten
cold with lemon juice squeezed on top.

ALMOND BLUEFISH HASH

2 cups COOKED BLUEFISH
1 1/2 cups COOKED, CUBED POTATOES
3 cups MEDIUM WHITE SAUCE
1 cup TOASTED SLIVERED ALMONDS
  BUTTER

PREHEAT OVEN TO 350°.

SAUTÉ ALMONDS IN BUTTER UNTIL GOLDEN.
MAKE WHITE SAUCE AND ADD BLUEFISH &
POTATOES. TRANSFER TO A SHALLOW BAKING dish.
Top WITH almonds. BAKE 15 MINUTES OR UNTIL
HEATED through.   SERVES 4-5

~ WHITE SAUCE

2 TBS BUTTER   1 CUP CREAM OR MILK
2 TBS FLOUR   SALT & PEPPER

MELT butter OVER low HEAT. Add FLOUR and stir
FOR A FEW MINUTES. SLOWLY Add milk and stir
UNTIL THICKENED, 5 OR 10 MINUTES. MAKES 1 CUP.

BAKED MARINATED BLUEFISH

2 FILLETS
1 CUP OLIVE OIL
2 CLOVES GARLIC - CRUSHED
1 ONION - SLICED

1 BAY LEAF
1 tsp SALT
1 tsp PEPPER
¼ CUP LEMON JUICE

DRY WHITE WINE

Lay fillets in shallow dish and cover with mixture of oil, garlic, onion, bay leaf, salt, pepper, lemon juice and enough wine to cover fish. Allow fish to marinate at least 12 hours.

Broil fish using marinade for basting.

BLUEFISH CAPERS

2 FILLETS
4 TBS BUTTER
1 TBS LEMON JUICE
2 tsps CAPERS

PREHEAT OVEN TO 350.°

Place Fillets in a greased baking dish and bake for 20 minutes or until fish Flakes easily with a fork. In a skillet melt butter until brown. Quickly add LEMON JUICE and CAPERS AND COOK for 15 SECONDS. Pour over FILLETS and serve.

BLUEFISH AU GRATIN

2 FILLETS
2 MEDIUM ONIONS - CHOPPED
1 CUP MUSHROOMS - THINLY SLICED
1 CUP SWISS CHEESE - GRATED
3 TBS BUTTER

PREHEAT OVEN TO 350°

Place fillets skin side down in a greased baking dish and Bake 20 minutes. Sauté onions and mushrooms in Butter, then place over baked fillets. Top with grated cheese and place under Broiler until cheese is melted and golden brown.

BUELLABASE - BOUILLABASE

1 FILLET - RAW OR COOKED
3 OR MORE KINDS OF FISH OR SHELLFISH
2 MEDIUM ONIONS - CHOPPED
2 CLOVES GARLIC - MINCED
1/4 CUP OLIVE OIL
3 TOMATOES - CHOPPED   1/2 CAN TOMATO PASTE
1/4 tsp: OREGANO, BASIL, THYME, SAGE, MARJORAM
1 1/2 QTS. FISH STOCK OR { 24 OZ. CLAM JUICE
                          { 24 OZ. WATER

Sauté onion and garlic in oil in a large pan. When golden add tomatoes, paste and herbs. Cook until tomatoes are soft. Then add remaining ingredients and simmer for 20 minutes (be sure shellfish are well scrubbed before adding). Cooking time will vary depending on the use of raw or cooked fish. Serve with crisp french Bread and grated Parmesan cheese.

OPEN-FACED SANDWICH

TOAST BREAD SLICES ON ONE SIDE. COVER UNTOASTED side with BLUEFISH SALAD (SEE RECIPE FOR EO'S BLUEFISH Salad - page 22, OMITTING THE ALFALFA SProuts).

SPREAD MAYONNAISE EVENLY OVER THE BLUEFISH SALAD. SHAKE GRATED PARMESAN CHEESE OVER MAYONNAISE and place UNDER BROILER UNTIL TOP is BROWNED and bubbly.

GOOBER BLUES

2 FILLETS

1 CUP COARSELY CHOPPED SALTED PEANUTS

1/4 CUP MELTED BUTTER

PREHEAT OVEN TO 375.°

PLACE FILLETS IN GREASED, SHALLOW CASSEROLE
DISH. COVER WITH CHOPPED PEANUTS. DRIBBLE
MELTED BUTTER OVER ALL. BAKE FOR 20-25
MINUTES. SERVE WITH FRIED BANANAS.

BLUES À L'ORANGE

2 FILLETS
BASTING SAUCE: ⅓ PART ORANGE JUICE
⅓ PART MELTED BUTTER
⅓ PART SOY SAUCE

PREPARE basting sauce. Place fillets, skin side down, on broiler pan. Baste generously with sauce. Grill under broiler for 20-25 minutes, basting occasionally with sauce.

LEFTOVER SAUCE is also good on BROILED CHICKEN.

Bluefish with Ginger and Scallions

2 FILLETS
1/2 - 3/4 cup soy sauce
1/4 cup fresh ginger - minced
OR 3 TBS ground ginger
1/2 cup scallions - chopped

PREHEAT OVEN TO 350°

marinate fillets in soy sauce for 10 minutes
each side. Then rub flesh with ginger and
scallions. Place fillets in greased baking
dish. Pour soy sauce over fillets and
bake 20 minutes or until done.

BLUE - AGREE

2 CUPS COOKED RICE
2 CUPS COOKED BLUEFISH - FLAKED
4 HARD COOKED EGGS - CHOPPED
2 TBS MINCED PARSLEY
1/2 CUP MELTED BUTTER

ADD TO THE HOT COOKED RICE THE REST OF THE
INGREDIENTS, EXCEPT THE BUTTER. PREHEAT IN
THE TOP OF A DOUBLE BOILER. ADD MELTED
BUTTER AND STIR IN WELL.

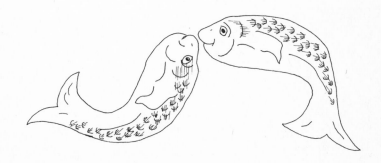

Bluefish with Shrimp Sauce

2 Fillets
1 Can cream of Shrimp Soup
1/3 cup Chopped Cooked Shrimp
OR 1 2 1/3 - 3 oz can of Tiny Shrimp
1/2 cup white wine

PREHEAT OVEN TO 350°

Place Fillets skin side down in a greased baking
dish and cover with remaining mixed ingredients,
including the Juice from the Lemon. Slice the
squeezed Lemon into thin HALF-Rounds and
decoratively place in a line on Fillets. Bake 25
minutes or until done.

Serve with Rice.

BAKED STUFFED BLUEFISH

2 large fillets or whole fish
2 cups bread crumbs *
1 large onion
4 TBS butter
1/2 lb. chopped mushrooms **

1/2 tsp thyme
1/4 cup chopped parsley
2 TBS chopped celery leaves
1 tsp salt
1 egg - beaten

PREHEAT OVEN TO 375°

Sauté onions in butter until soft. Add the other ingredients and mix well. Stuff the bluefish by placing one fillet over the other. Place in a greased baking dish and bake for 40 minutes or until fish flakes easily with a fork.

* or Pepperidge farms - Arnold stuffing
** try substituting oysters or shrimp

BLUEFISH - SWEDISH STYLE

2 FILLETS
2 CUPS MEDIUM CREAM SAUCE
  DILL

PREHEAT OVEN TO 350.°

BAKE THE FILLETS IN OVEN FOR 20-25 MINUTES OR
UNTIL JUST TENDER. MEANWHILE MAKE A MEDIUM
CREAM SAUCE. ADD THE FINELY CHOPPED FRESH DILL
(OR DRIED DILL WEED) VERY GENEROUSLY. BE SURE TO
MAKE IT TASTE 'DILLY.' SERVE WITH A LIGHT
COATING OF THE SAUCE. PLACE THE REMAINING IN A
DISH AND SERVE SEPARATELY.

CREAM SAUCE

3 TBS BUTTER   1 CUP CREAM
3 TBS FLOUR   SALT & PEPPER

MELT BUTTER OVER LOW HEAT. ADD FLOUR & STIR A MOMENT.
SLOWLY ADD MILK & STIR UNTIL THICKENED.

FABULOUS MARINATED BLUEFISH
AND
COLD PASTA BLUEFISH SALAD

The following recipes are Chef Vannerson's favorites. The first makes a fabulous marinated bluefish, and the second is a salad using the leftover marinade and leftover bluefish. She says that they are "great for a crowd, and both can be made ahead of time."

2 BLUEFISH FILLETS (OR MORE DEPENDING ON SIZE)
1 RED ONION, SLICED
2 TOMATOES, SLICED

~ MARINADE

1 CUP OLIVE OIL
1/2 CUP RED WINE VINEGAR
1/2 CUP DIJON MUSTARD
2 TABLESPOONS SUGAR

1 TEASPOON SALT
4 TABLESPOONS CHOPPED PARSLEY
1 1/2 TEASPOONS FRESH GROUND PEPPER

3/4 CUP VODKA OR GIN (OMIT IF MAKING ONLY THE SALAD)

MIX All the INGREDIENTS FOR MARINADE EXCEPT the VODKA or GIN. PUREE IN blENDEr. STIR IN VODKA OR GIN.

PLACE the FILLETS, SKIN SIDE DOWN, IN PYREX BOWl (NOT METAL) AND POUR MARINADE OVER them. COVER WITH PlASTIC WRAP AND REFRIGERATE FOR two to Four Hours. TURN the FISH OVER IN the MARINADE EVERY HOUR OR SO.

REMOVE FILLETS, RESERVING the MARINADE (FOR USE IN ACCOMPANYING RECIPE), AND PlACE them SKIN SIDE DOWN ON A BROiling PAN that has been lINED WITH FOIL.

BROil FOR FIVE MINUTES AT 5-6 INCHES From HEAT. REMOVE AND TOP WITH the SlICED tOMATOES AND RED ONION. BROil AGAIN UNTIl FISH IS FlAKED AND VEGETABlES ARE COOKED. SPRINKlE WITH CHOPPED PARSLEY.   SERVES 4.

COLD PASTA BLUEFISH SALAD

1 POUND PASTA IN DIFFERENT SHAPES
BLUEFISH MARINADE
LEFTOVER MARINATED BLUEFISH
2 TABLESPOONS CAPERS
4 TABLESPOONS CHOPPED PARSLEY
2 TABLESPOONS CHOPPED CHIVES
1 CUP CHERRY TOMATOES, QUARTERED
1 TABLESPOON CHOPPED SUN-DRIED TOMATOES
1/2 CUP CHOPPED SEEDED CUCUMBER   (OPTIONAL)
MINCED FRESH PARSLEY FOR GARNISH

COOK A VARIETY OF PASTA SHAPES, ALL
APPROXIMATELY THE SAME SIZE (ZITI, SPIRALS,
SHELLS, PINWHEELS, ETC.). COOK UNTIL _AL DENTE_,
THEN WHILE STILL WARM, TOSS WITH THE
BLUEFISH MARINADE. USE A GENEROUS
AMOUNT OF THE MARINADE, AS THE PASTA
SHOULD NOT BE DRY.

TOSS WITH the bluefish, the capers, the chopped parsley, the chives, the tomatoes, AND the cucumber. Place in refrigerator FOR one Hour. Serve on lettuce with Fresh parsley (OR water- cress) AND LEMON WEDGES.

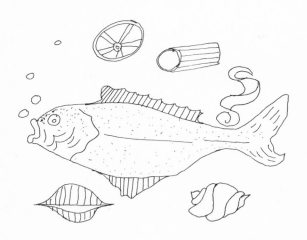

From the Thisyie Restaurant, Nantucket; SHARON Vannerson, Chef De Cuisine.

BAKED BLUEFISH
(A GAY HEAD RECIPE)

4 to 6 PORTIONS

½ loaf DAY-old Home-styIE Bread, cruSTS Removed

1½ teaspoons poultry seasoning

½ cup ground SAH Pork

¼ teaspoon Freshly ground pepper

1 Tablespoon melted Butter

½ cup boiling WATER

4 BLuEfish FilleTS, a total of approximately 3 pounds

8 lemon slices

8 thin slices SAH Pork

Additional lemon slices (optional)

PARsLey sprigs

PreheaT OVEN to 375°F.

Prepare the breAD stuffing As Follows: Cut the bread into ½-inch Cubes. In a mixing bowl combine the breaD, poultry seasoning, ground SALT pork, pepper, and melted butter. Using a Fork For mixing, gradually add the boiling WATER, lifting and combining all ingredients, until properly moistened. Spread The stuffing

Equally on two of the bluefish fillets; cover with the remaining fillets. Place 8 lemon slices on the fish, then the thin salt pork slices.

BAKE the fish in a shallow casserole or baking dish (try lining with aluminum foil for easy cleanup) about 25 minutes. The fish is ready for the table when it flakes easily when pierced with a fork. Serve with additional lemon slices, if desired, and garnish with parsley sprigs.

From the martha's vineyard cook book (The globe Pequot Press, 1971) by Louise Tate King and Jean Stewart Wexler.

SPICY BLUEFISH WITH SUMMER SAVORY

6 very small Bluefish Fillets
Flour
Enough Oil to saute
SALT, Pepper, Fresh summer SAVORY TO TASTE

~ SAUCE

3 TABLESPOONS Olive Oil   8 ounces White WINE
1 MEDIUM-SIZED ONION, DICED   8 ounces Clam Juice
                                 (MORE MAY BE NEEDED)
1 JALAPEÑO PEPPER, DICED   1 bAY LEAF
28 OUNCES CANNED TOMATOES IN JUICE, OR Fresh
          SUMMER TOMATOES

~ GARNISH

1 Yellow bell PEPPER
1 GREEN bell PEPPER
1 RED bell PEPPER
2 CUPS FIRM mushrooms

To make Sauce, saute ONION AND JalapEÑO

pepper in the 3 tablespoons of oil for a few minutes. Add white wine and simmer over medium heat for 5 minutes. Add 8 ounces clam juice, tomatoes, and bay leaf; simmer for 45 minutes. Puree sauce through a food mill. The sauce should be just thick enough to cover the fish lightly. If it is too thick, lighten it with more clam juice or white wine. If too thin, simmer until it is reduced to the DESIRED CONSISTENCY.

- To make garnish, ROAST the peppers—Rub them with a little olive oil and put them under a very hot broiler and char the skin until black. Rub skin off under running water. Discard seeds and stems. Cut mushrooms & peppers into 1/4" dice.

- To complete the dish, lightly dredge bluefish in flour. Put some oil in a frying pan,

Enough to cover the bottom. ADD BLUEFISH.
Saute, then place on platter and keep
warm. Add DICED mushrooms to the oil,
adding extra oil if needed, then ADD
peppers. SEASON generously with salt,
pepper, AND fresh summer savory. LADLE
warm sauce across fish, then spoon
garnish on top.

SERVES 6

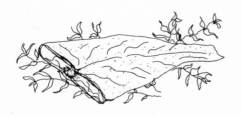

From Michael Shannon's CLUB CAR RESTaurant,
NANTUCKET (FRANK LUCAS, sous-chef).

North Wharf Fish House Stew

2 8-ounce bluefish fillets, diced
1 pound scallops *
1 pound langostinos *
1 cup chopped celery
1 cup chopped carrot
1 cup chopped onion
1/4 teaspoon cayenne pepper
1/4 teaspoon black pepper
pinch of basil
tamari to taste
3 tablespoons olive oil
1 quart fresh fish stock (see page 49)
1 quart clam broth
1 quart canned whole peeled tomatoes,
        broken up.
1 cup prepared marinara sauce
6 medium-size boiled new potatoes, diced

In a heavy stew pot, sauté in the olive
oil the celery, the carrots, the onion. Add

the CAYENNE AND black PEPPER, the BASIL,
AND the XAMARI.
ADD the Fish STOCK, the Clam broth, the
tomatoes, AND the MARINARA sauce. Simmer
UNTIL All the Vegetables ARE tender.
TO SERVE, Saute the diced fresh bluefish,
fresh scallops, langostinos* and boiled
New POTATOES AND Add to EACH PORTION
OF stew bASE.

*
The SCAllops AND langostinos CAN be
replaced by AN EQUIVALENT AMOUNT OF other
Fish or shellfish.

FROM ROb Mitchell's NORTH WHARF
Fish House, NANTUCKET.

BLUEFISH WITH APPLES

4 6-ounce bluefish fillets

3 TABLESPOONS UNSALTED BUTTER

1 SMALL RED ONION, THINLY SLICED

1 TART APPLE, PEELED AND THINLY SLICED

1/2 CUP QUICK FISH STOCK (SEE BELOW)

1/3 CUP HEAVY CREAM

1 to 2 TABLESPOONS POMMERY MUSTARD (OR ANY COARSE-GRAINED MUSTARD)

FRESH ITALIAN PARSLEY OR WATERCRESS FOR GARNISH

1. IF YOU ARE PORTIONING THE FISH, CUT IT INTO 4 EQUAL PORTIONS, CUTTING SLIGHTLY ON THE DIAGONAL. DISCARD 2 to 3 INCHES OF THE TAIL END. REMOVE ANY BONES. IF THERE IS ANY SKIN ON THE FILLETS, LEAVE IT ON.

2. REDUCE THE FISH STOCK TO 1/4 CUP IN A

1- QUART STAINLESS STEEL SAUCEPAN. SET ASIDE.

3. PREHEAT A broiler.

4. Butter the bluefish with 1 TABLESPOON Butter AND place on AN OILED BROILER PAN. BROIL the Fish 6 INCHES FROM the HEAT UNTIL the top OF THE FILLETS IS A light GOLDEN BROWN. TO CHECK FOR DONENESS, INSERT A SMALL SHARP KNIFE INTO the thickest PART OF EACH FILLET. IF THE FISH IS NOT COOKED through, but ALREADY brown, turN OFF THE broiler AND BAKE AT 350 DEGREES FOR 3 to 6 MINUTES UNTIL DONE.

5. MEANWHILE, heAT 2 TableSpooNs butter IN A 12- INCH Saute PaN. Add the ONION AND TOSS OVer high heAT UNTIL SOFT. Add the APPLES AND TOSS For 3 MINUTES. Place ON A SERVING PLATTER AND

KEEP WARM.

6. Add the REDUCED FISH STOCK to the SAUTE PAN. WHISK IN 1 TABLESPOON MUSTARD AND REDUCE the SAUCE to A MEDIUM SYRUPY CONSISTENCY. Add the CREAM AND REDUCE UNTIL the SAUCE is thick Enough to COAT A SPOON. ADD SALT, Freshly ground PEPPER, and more mustard to taste.

7. WHEN you remove the FILLETS From the broiler pan, do NOT be concerned IF the SKIN stays stuck to the pan. Place the FILLETS over the ONION-APPLE mixture AND top with the SAUCE. GARNISH WITH ITALIAN PARSLEY or WATERCRESS.
SERVES 4.

FROM <u>ANOTHER</u> <u>SEASON</u> <u>COOKBOOK</u> (THE GLOBE PEQUOT PRESS, 1986) by ODETTE J. BERY, CHEF/OWNER OF ANOTHER SEASON RESTAURANT IN BOSTON.

～ QUICK FISH STOCK
(FOR USE IN BLUEFISH WITH APPLES)

1 pound haddock, COD, OR pollock
2 TABLESPOONS UNSALTED BUTTER
1 SMALL ONION, thinly SLICED
1 CELERY STALK, thinly SLICED
1/2 bAY LEAF
PINCH OF MACE (OPTIONAL)
FEW SPRIGS PARSLEY (OPTIONAL)
1 CUP White WINE
4 CUPS COLD WATER

1. HEAT the butter IN A 2-3-QUART STAINLESS STEEL OR ENAMEL PAN. (DO NOT USE AN ALUMINUM PAN.) ADD the ONION AND CELERY. GENTLY SAUTE over MEDIUM heAT UNTIL SOFT, being CAREFUL NOT TO BROWN. ADD Fish, bAY LEAF, MACE, PARSLEY, WINE, AND WATER. Bring TO A BOIL AND BOIL FOR 5 MINUTES, then SKIM OFF AND DISCARD ANY FOAM.

2. Gently simmer, uncovered, for 45 minutes, then strain through a fine sieve.
(your cats, if you have any, will love the
fish; if not, discard.)

3. If there are a lot of particies in the
stock, run it through a couple of layers
of cheesecloth to remove them. The stock
may be refrigerated 3 to 4 days. Keep
fat covering on top of stock. It may
also be frozen.

Yields 1 quart.

From ANOTHER SEASON COOKBOOK (The
Globe Pequot Press, 1986) by ODETTE
J. Bery.

BLUEFISH MOLLY'S WAY

2 SLICES BLUEFISH 8 to 10 OUNCES EACH, WITH SKIN
1/2 CUP SOUR CREAM
2 TEASPOONS WHITE HORSERADISH
1/2 CUP MAYONNAISE
DASH TABASCO SAUCE
DASH WORCESTERSHIRE SAUCE
1/4 TEASPOON GROUND DILL
1 LEMON, CUT IN HALF
FRESH DILL FOR GARNISH

IN A SMALL MIXING BOWL, BEAT SOUR CREAM,
HORSERADISH, MAYONNAISE, TABASCO AND
WORCESTERSHIRE SAUCES, AND GROUND DILL.
PLACE FISH ON BROILER PAN, SKIN SIDE DOWN.
SQUEEZE LEMON HALVES OVER FISH, THEN
SPREAD SAUCE EVENLY OVER EACH PIECE.
WITH FISH ABOUT 8 INCHES FROM BROILER,
HEAT FOR 15 MINUTES. GARNISH WITH FRESH

DILL.

SERVES 4

FROM ENTREE LU CATERING COMPANY,
ESSEX, CONNECTICUT.

BEIGNETS DE BLUEFISH

2 POUNDS bluefish FILLEYS
1 POUND TOMATOES, PEELED
2 EGGS
FLOUR, SALT, PEPPER
2 TABLESPOONS OLIVE OIL
1 CUP FISH STOCK

A MARINADE
2 CUPS WATER
1 TABLESPOON CORIANDER SEED
4 CLOVES GARLIC
1 TABLESPOON CUMIN
3 TABLESPOONS OLIVE OIL

2 HOT PEPPERS
1 WHOLE LEMON PEEL
PINCH OF SAFFRON
2 TABLESPOONS GRATED GINGER
6 MINT LEAVES

Blend MARINADE INGREDIENTS XOGEther. CUX
FISH INXO thick SCALOPPINES AND place IN
MARINADE. REFRIGERATE FOR A FEW HOURS.

TO MAKE TOMATO SAUCE, SAUTE TOMATOES
IN 1 TABLESPOON OLIVE OIL UNTIL COOKED.
ADD FISH STOCK, 1 CUP MARINADE, AND
SALT TO TASTE. COOK AN ADDITIONAL 15
MINUTES. PUREE IN BLENDER. KEEP WARM.

REMOVE FISH FROM MARINADE AND ADD
SALT AND PEPPER. DIP IN FLOUR, THEN IN
BEATEN EGGS. SAUTE IN 1 TABLESPOON OLIVE
OIL FOR 2 MINUTES ON EACH SIDE.

SERVE WITH TOMATO SAUCE.

FROM THE CHANTICLEER RESTAURANT,
NANTUCKET — JEAN CHARLES BERRUET,
CHEF/PROPRIETOR.

BLUEFISH WITH ORANGE SAUCE

4 6-ounce bluefish fillets (skin on)
4 tablespoons vegetable oil
2 medium onions, very finely sliced
12 Italian parsley sprigs
1 teaspoon grated orange rind (zest)
2 to 4 tablespoons lemon juice
1/4 cup fresh orange juice
salt and pepper

Remove any bones from the bluefish.
Just before serving, preheat a broiler
and adjust so that the pan will be 6
inches from the heat.
Brush a broiler pan and bluefish with a
little oil and place under the broiler.
While the fish is broiling, heat the 4
teaspoons of vegetable oil in a 10 or 12

INCH STAINLESS STEEL SAUTE PAN. ADD THE
ONIONS AND SAUTE UNTIL THEY ARE
CLEAR BUT STILL SLIGHTLY CRISP. ARRANGE
HALF THE ONIONS ON 4 DINNER PLATES
AND ARRANGE THE ITALIAN PARSLEY OVER
THE ONIONS.

ADD 2 TABLESPOONS LEMON JUICE, THE
ORANGE JUICE, AND THE ORANGE ZEST
WITH THE REMAINING ONIONS IN THE SAUTE
PAN AND REDUCE OVER A MEDIUM HEAT FOR
3 TO 5 MINUTES UNTIL THE MIXTURE IS OF
A SLIGHTLY SYRUPY CONSISTENCY. ADD SALT
AND FRESHLY GROUND BLACK PEPPER TO TASTE
AND MORE LEMON JUICE TO TASTE IF DESIRED.
WHILE THE SAUCE IS REDUCING, CHECK THE
BLUEFISH DONENESS BY INSERTING A SMALL
SHARP KNIFE INTO THE THICKEST PART OF
THE FISH. IF THE BLUEFISH IS NOT COOKED
BUT ALREADY GOLDEN BROWN, FINISH COOKING

by BAKING AT 375 DEGREES FOR ANOTHER
3 to 7 MINUTES.
WHEN the BLUEFISH IS COOKED, ARrANGE
OUER the ONIONS AND SPOON the SOUCE
OUER EACH FiileYs. SERUE IMMEDIATELY.

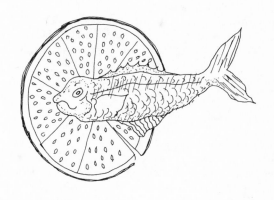

From ANOther SEASON RESYAUrANT IN
BOSYON (ODETTE BErY. CheF/OWner).

BLUEFISH SOUP

8 OUNCES SKINLESS
 bluefish FILLET, IN bite-
 SIZED PIECES

4 SLICES BACON, DICED

1 TABLESPOON butter

1/2 CUP CHOPPED ONION

1 QUART OF
 half WATER, half
CLAM JUICE, OR PLAIN WATER

2 CUPS CHOPPED CELERY
(SAVE 1 TABLESPOON OF LEAVES)

PINCH OF DRIED thyme

1/2 teaspoon SALT

3 to 4 turns Freshly
 ground pepper

1 CUP heavy CREAM

1/2 CUP PEELED, SEEDED,
 AND DICED TOMATOES

1 TABLESPOON MINCED
 FRESH PARSLEY

1. Fry BACON IN butter IN A THICK - bottomED
4-QUART SAUCEPAN OR STOCK POT to RENDER
THE FAT. WHEN BACON IS CRISP, REMOVE half
OF IT, blot ON PAPER towels, AND reserve.
LEAVE bacon FAT AND the other half OF
The bacon IN The PAN.

2. ADD The ONIONS   AND SAUTE UNTIL

lightly browned. ADD Fish STOCK or other liquid, CELERY, thyme, SALT, AND PEPPER. Simmer, COVERED, 30 to 35 MINUTES, OR UNTIL CELERY IS TENDER.

3. PLACE CONTENTS OF PAN INTO WORK BOWL OF FOOD PROCESSOR, IN TWO BATCHES IF NECESSARY, AND WORK UNTIL smooth.

4. RETURN to PAN AND bring to A boil, then lower heat TO Simmer AND ADD CREAM. COOK OVER low heat 5 MINUTES. ADD TOMATOES AND PARSLEY AND Then FISH. SIMMER 3 to 4 MINUTES, AND CORRECT the SEASONING.

5. LADLE the SOUP INTO INDIVIDUAL SOUP PLATES or INTO A SOUP TUREEN. ADD bACON biTS AND CELERY LEAVES AS garnish.

SERVES 4.

FROM SEAFOOD AS WE LIKE IT (The GLOBE PEQUOT PRESS, 1985) by ANTHONY SPINAZZOLA AND JEAN-JACQUES PAIMBLANC. JEAN-JACQUES IS CURRENTLY DIRECTOR OF RESEARCH AND DEVELOPMENT AND EXECUTIVE CHEF FOR THE LEGAL SEAFOODS RESTAURANTS IN THE BOSTON AREA.

BLUEFISH PROVENÇALE
(BAKED WITH AROMATIC HERBS AND SEASONINGS)

4 PORTIONS

4—5-pound bluefish, CLEANED AND CUT INTO
2-INCH-thick slices ('bone IN)

MARINADE

1 CUP OlIVE OR VEGETABLE
OIL

1/2 CUP RED WINE VINEGAR

1 TABLESPOON LEMON JUICE

1 teaspoon SALT

1/4 teaspoon Freshly
ground Pepper

2 Cloves GARLIC,
MINCED FINE

PLACE the bluefish slices IN A shallow
CONTAINER; COMBINE the 1 CUP OIl, VINEGAR,
lemon juice, 1 teaspoon SALT, PEPPER, AND
The 2 MINCED GARlic cloves and pour
over the Fish. MARINATE the Fish IN This
mixture two to three hours, turning
OCCASIONALLY. REFRIGERATION IS NOT REQUIRED.

PREHEAT OVEN TO 450°F.

Remove fish from marinade; dry it thoroughly with paper towels. Discard marinade.

2 tablespoons butter

2 tablespoons olive or vegetable oil

1 cup onions, thinly sliced

3 cups fresh tomatoes, cut in chunks (canned may be substituted)

2 cloves garlic, minced fine

1 teaspoon salt

1/4 teaspoon freshly ground pepper

1 cup dry white wine

4 tablespoons tomato paste

2 beef bouillon cubes

1/2 cup chopped parsley

1/2 teaspoon dried thyme

SCANT teaspoon dried oregano

Over high heat melt the butter with the oil in a heavy skillet until the butter foam subsides. Quickly brown the fish on both sides, allowing 2 to 3 minutes per side. Remove from skillet and arrange in a shallow flameproof baking dish.

In the same skillet, over moderate

heat, cook the onions until transparent.
Add a little more butter or oil if the onions
demand it. Add the tomatoes, the remaining
2 cloves minced garlic, the remaining
teaspoon salt, pepper, wine, tomato paste,
bouillon cubes, 1/4 cup of the chopped
parsley, thyme, and oregano. Cook over
high heat, stirring frequently, about 10
minutes, allowing the liquids to evaporate
sufficiently so that sauce is thickened
slightly.

Pour the sauce over the bluefish slices,
sprinkle with the remaining 1/4 cup
chopped parsley, cover the dish tightly
with foil, and bake 15 to 20 minutes, or
until the fish flakes easily when
pierced with a fork.

Transfer the fish to a heated platter;
keep warm. Place the baking dish with

Its remaining sauce over high heat and boil rapidly, stirring constantly, until about 2 cups of sauce remain. Pour sauce over fish slices and serve immediately.

NOTE: The sauce may be thickened slightly with a paste of 1 tablespoon flour mixed with 1 tablespoon softened butter.

From The MARTHA'S VINEYARD COOKBOOK (The Globe Pequot Press, 1971) by LOUISE TATE KING AND JEAN STEWART WEXLER.

BLOUP

8 quahogs

½ gallon water

1 Tablespoon bacon drippings

1 large diced onion

5 garlic cloves, smashed

10 summer tomatoes, peeled, seeded, and chopped

¼ cup fresh basil, finely chopped

1 Tablespoon chopped parsley

1 Tablespoon sugar

Pinch of thyme

Salt & pepper to taste

2 cloves

1 Bay leaf

1 pound bluefish cut into 1" cubes

Wash quahogs; put into soup pot with 1 quart of water. Cover and steam until opened. Reserve stock; remove meat from shell and chop and reserve. In heavy-bottomed soup pot, melt bacon drippings and add chopped onion and garlic. Sauté until translucent. Add chopped tomatoes, quahog juice, seasonings, and remainder of water. Simmer 1 hour. Add bluefish cubes. Simmer for 15 minutes. Add guahog meat, return to simmer, and serve.

This recipe is exceptional in late August when the blues are thick, the tomatoes are ripe, basil is abundant, and the nights have a faint whisper of autumn.

From E. J. Harvey's The Island Restaurant, Nantucket.

BLUEFISH DIJONAISE

2 8-OUNCE BLUEFISH FILLETS
2 TABLESPOONS PREPARED HORSERADISH
2 TABLESPOONS DIJON MUSTARD
2 TABLESPOONS MAYONNAISE
1 TEASPOON OLD BAY SEASONING
½ CUP BREADCRUMBS — SEASONED

MIX HORSERADISH, MAYONNAISE, AND MUSTARD.
COAT THE BLUEFISH FILLETS WITH THE MIXTURE,
THEN LIGHTLY COAT WITH A MIXTURE OF THE
OLD BAY SEASONING AND THE BREADCRUMBS.
BAKE IN A 350-DEGREE OVEN FOR 20
MINUTES OR UNTIL FISH IS COOKED.
SERVES 2.

From Fiddlers SEAFood RESTAURANT,
Chester, Connecticut (Donald Lloyd, Chef).

BROILED BLUEFISH BELLA VISTA

2   8-ounce bluefish fillets
6   strips bacon, sliced
1   small onion, julienned
1   green pepper, julienned
2   ripe tomatoes, peeled and diced
1/2 teaspoon chopped garlic
1/2 cup white wine
1   stick butter
1   lemon, cut in half

Sauté bacon. When half cooked, add onions, peppers, and tomatoes. Cook until onions and peppers are soft, then add garlic, 1/4 cup white wine, 1/2 stick butter, and juice from squeezed 1/2 lemon. Simmer 3 to 5 minutes.

Place bluefish in pan and top with 1/2

stick melted butter and 1/4 cup white
wine. Squeeze lemon half over fish.
Broil 8 to 10 minutes.

When done, top bluefish with sauce
and serve with rice.

SERVES 2

From the MAD HATTER RESTAURANT,
NANTUCKET.

Sauces

~ TOMATO - YOGURT

2 cups yogurt
1 TBS ONION - FINEly MINCED
3 TBS TOMATO SAUCE
3 TBS KETCHUP
1/2 tsp Sugar
1/2 tsp curry Powder
    SALT and PEPPER

MIX ALL INGREDIENTS AND REFRIGERATE UNTIL
SERVED.

~ SOUR CREAM AND DILL SAUCE

1/2 cup Sour CREAM or YOGURT
    DILL - TO TASTE

MIX Sour CREAM and DILL and A PINCH Of SALT.

~ GEOFF'S WHITE SAUCE FOR SMOKED FISH

2 TBS BUTTER	1 tsp DILL
1 TBS FLOUR	2 TBS VINEGAR
2 1/2 CUPS MILK	1 TBS HORSERADISH
1 tsp SALT	1/2 tsp GROUND GINGER
1 tsp PEPPER	1 tBS MAYONNAISE

MELT BUTTER UNTIL BUBBLING, STIR IN FLOUR
and COOK FOR A FEW MINUTES. GRADUALLY ADD
MILK, STIRRING UNTIL SAUCE IS SMOOTH and
THICKENED. ADD REMAINING INGREDIENTS. SERVE
OVER SMOKED BLUEFISH ON TOAST OR ON A
MIXTURE OF FLAKED, SMOKED FISH and SCRAMBLED
EGGS.

~ HOLLANDAISE

3 EGG YOLKS
1/4 CUP LEMON JUICE
1/4 tsp SALT
1/2 CUP BUTTER
  DASH OF PAPRIKA
  DASH OF CAYENNE PEPPER

PUT ALL INGREDIENTS, EXCEPT THE butter, INTO
A blENDER AND mix bRIEFLY. MELT butter
UNTIL it bEGINS to bubble. GRADUALLY ADD
butter to the blENDER WHILE THE motor is
runNING. mix UNTIL smooth AND Thick.

~ SORREL SAUCE

¼ CUP butter
¼ CUP PARMESAN CHEESE
¼ CUP OLIVE OIL
¼ CUP PINE NUTS or SMALL AMOUNT OF PEANUTS
4 sprigs PARSLEY
1 CLOVE garlic
1 CUP SORREL LEAVES

COMBINE ALL ingredients IN blender AND whirl
UNTIL FINELY CHOPPED. SERVE AT ROOM temper-
ATURE.   CAN be refrigerated, but ALLOW TO
return to ROOM temperature TO SERVE.
MAKES About 1 CUP.

∼ GREEN SAUCE

1 CLOVE GARLIC	2 tsp CAPERS
4 TBS PARSLEY	1 TBS PICKLE JUICE
2 ANCHOVIES	1 TBS VINEGAR
3 mushrooms	1/2 - 3/4 CUP OLIVE OIL
1 SMALL DILL PICKLE	1 EGG YOLK - HARD BOILED
1 SMALL SCALLION	

1 SMALL STRIP OF GREEN OR RED PEPPER
1 SMALL POTATO, PEELED and BOILED

FINELY CHOP and MASH TOGETHER ALL INGREDIENTS,
EXCEPT OIL, INTO A COARSE PASTE. FLOAT SOME
OIL ON TOP TO KEEP. PLACE IN A COOL SPOT,
UNREFRIGERATED AND COVERED. Add more oil AS
NECESSARY.

~ ED'S TOMATO SAUCE FOR BAKED BLUEFISH

2 CUPS TOMATO SAUCE
2 ONIONS - CHOPPED
1 TBS CHOPPED DILL
1/2 tsp MINCED GARLIC
1/2 tsp FRESHLY GROUND PEPPER
2 TBS OLIVE OIL
2 TBS VINEGAR
1 TBS MIXED HERBS - OREGANO, BASIL, ROSEMARY
1/2 CUP SOUR CREAM
  PARSLEY
2 WHOLE FRESH TOMATOES - QUARTERED

SIMMER ALL INGREDIENTS, EXCEPT SOUR CREAM, IN COVERED SAUCE PAN FOR 40 MINUTES. ADD THE SOUR CREAM TO THE HOT SAUCE AND POUR OVER HOT BAKED BLUEFISH. GARNISH WITH PARSLEY.

∿ MUSTARD - DILL SAUCE

1 CUP DIJON MUSTARD - 8 oz JAR
1/3 CUP YOGURT or SOUR CREAM
1/3 CUP SUGAR
1/3 CUP WHITE VINEGAR
1 CUP OLIVE or VEG. OIL
1 CUP CHOPPED FRESH DILL
 SALT and PEPPER

MIX ALL INGREDIENTS EXCEPT OIL and DILL.
GRADUALLY STIR IN OIL UNTIL SMOOTH. THEN
STIR IN DILL. REFRIGERATE UNTIL SERVED.

~ garlic MAYONNAISE

3 CLOVES garlic – FINELY chopped
2 EGGS
6 TBS LEMON JUICE
½ tsp EACH SALT and PEPPER
1½ CUP OLIVE OIL

BLEND ALL INGREDIENTS, EXCEPT OIL, IN BLENDER.
THEN gradually POUR IN OIL UNTIL THE mixture is
smooth AND thickENED, BUT MORE LIQUID than
regular MAYONNAISE, AS you wish it as A
SAUCE. COVER & REFRIGERATE UNTIL SERVED.

OR simply BLEND garlic with your FAVORITE
STORE – BOUGHT MAYONNAISE.

∿ BROWN BUTTER AND CAPERS

HEAT BUTTER UNTIL BROWNED. Add 2 tsp CAPERS
and 1 TBS LEMON JUICE. HEAT QUICKLY. POUR
OVER FILLETS.

∿ BUTTERS

ADD TO SOFTENED BUTTER ANY HERB - TARRAGON,
ROSEMARY, CHIVES, PARSLEY, ETC. - TO YOUR
TASTE.

Index to Recipes

Recipes for sauces begin on page 97.